TOP TEN RULES FOR WINNING: THE HABITS OF JOSEPH STALIN

*TOP 10 RULES FROM HIGHLY SUCCESSFUL PEOPLE ON HOW TO WIN IN BUSINESS, CAREERS, THE CORPORATE WORLD, AND ELSEWHERE*

ERNEST EDSEL

I0466610

Copyright (c) 2024 Ernest M. Edsel

All Rights Reserved.

TOP TEN RULES FOR WINNING: THE HABITS OF JOSEF STALIN.

*TOP 10 RULES FROM HIGHLY SUCCESSFUL PEOPLE ON HOW TO WIN IN BUSINESS, CAREERS, THE CORPORATE WORLD, AND ELSEWHERE*

First Edition, 2024.

EXCELSIOR MEDIA
SILOAM SPRINGS, MISSOURI

All rights reserved. No part of this book may be reproduced or transmitted in any form or by any means, graphic, electronic, or mechanical, including photocopying, recording, taking, or by any information storage retrieval system, without the permission in writing from the publisher.

An electronic format of this book has been specially priced to introduce readers to the best of crime fiction.

FIRST U.S. EDITION.

Please send book and author inquiries to:
Ms. Sofia de la Garza
TorreyAgency@outlook.com

Printed and Manufactured in the United States of America

DEDICATION

To Prof. Stephen Covey. You kindly encouraged me on finding rules for winning (whether from good or bad people). Meeting you was one of many benefits when I moved to Utah, from 1993 to 1995, to do venture capital. Though gone, you left behind quite a legacy in management, starting with your bestseller, *The 7 Habits of Highly Effective People*. You always understood the difference between effective and successful. They are not the same. Their difference is the reason for this book.

To Catherine Perebinossoff. You taught me that careers, business, and finance need big and deep thinking to win. I fondly remember our visits to Lazard Frères. As the doyenne of Citibank, you always have the best salon in Manhattan.

To Veronica Winwood. You taught me that priorities are all that matter in life and the corporate world. I will always admire how you put family first.

To San Simeon. These rules are for you.

To Louis E. Saenz de Santamaría. Your mentoring and friendship were priceless. Ditto your mentoring and friendship for my parents. Thank you for sharing the secrets of your success as a top executive at Johnson & Johnson, Revlon, Warner-Lambert, Richardson-Merrell (Vicks), and other companies.

# INTRODUCTION

Who should read this book?

This book is for people who are driven to win but also very busy. In other words, a VBP (Very Busy Person). Their careers and work are demanding. The VBP also has to deal with time-consuming issues that life throws at all of us: family responsibilities; school and other education; health issues; etc.

This book is also for anyone whose career or business needs a turbocharged boost (NATB).

If you're a VBP or NATB, then this book is for you. Why?

Because you need a way to quickly get as many useful career tips as possible. No business or law school, or Ph.D. program, will teach you any of the personal habits in this book that are proven and needed to win.

Even if you're lucky enough to have unlimited access to the best of experienced mentors, they will only have success in their limited or narrow field of expertise. This book gives you access to other people whose habits took them to great success in their chosen field of expertise.

To win in life, you need to learn and use the "Top 10 Rules" that have been proven to help a real person win at work or in their career, business, or specialized activity. The rules also apply to anyone who works in the three greatest swamps and jungles of all time: politics; government; and, big business or the corporate world.

The rules will also help turbocharge a stalled career or business or a new start in a career or business.

I've used all of these rules to win in life, and when I broke the rules, or did not use them, I lost big time.

What's the book about?

This book is a nutshell summary of the Top 10 habits that highly successful people used to a great advantage in their careers. In this case it's the dictator Joseph Stalin.

Who is Joseph Stalin?

Stalin was born in 1878 to poverty under the Czars of Russia. His birthplace was Georgia, a rugged and beautiful region of south Russia where the mountains of the Caucasus rise by the Black Sea. As a Georgian in the Russia Empire, he belonged to an ethnic minority. Russian was his second language, which he spoke with a thick Georgian accent his whole life. He wanted to be a priest and later a professor.

After dropping out of seminary, where he studied to be a priest, his only paying job for a short time was as a "weatherman." Basically, he was an observer taking notes at a weather station. But the job taught him to watch and wait, in silence and with patience, for signs of bigger things to come, like wind speed and wind direction to predict storms.

Stalin joined the underground opposition to the government. The Czar jailed and exiled him to distant villages for revolutionary propaganda and terrorist activities, including a deadly bank robbery.

Using his Top Ten Rules, Stalin outsmarted all of his rivals and enemies. Until his death in 1953, he ruthlessly ruled over communist Russia for more than 30 years, ever since 1922, when he started taking over from Lenin. Tens of millions died thanks to his orders and policies. Stalin led Russia to victory in World War II. The great dictator changed Russia from a backward agrarian nation into a modern industrial and military power.

Stalin had ten habits that made him a highly successful dictator, politician, conspirator, economic and war planner, people manager, author, and editor of newspapers and books. Like me, you can find out about his ten habits by carefully studying his life.

Each of Stalin's rules and habits sharpen and strengthen his other rules and habits. The rules are closely related and self-fulfilling. If you do one, then you can do the other.

I've read the ten best Stalin books with a total 6,385 pages. Over the years, I've read, re-read, and marked-up the ten books on Stalin and the ten habits that made him win.

I also read new books that come out on him all the time now that more historians have access to once-classified files in Russia.

And, I'm waiting for Prof. Kotkin to finish writing his third volume on Stalin. Since the 1980s, I've also attended lectures, seminars, and conferences on Stalin, including those by Prof. Kotkin, one of the top Stalin historians.

You can read all or some of the 6,385 pages from the books that I studied. Or, you can read this nutshell summary of his ten habits that I have summarized for you from the following ten books:

- 976 pages of *Stalin: Paradoxes of Power, 1878–1928* (Vol. I), by Princeton historian Stephen Kotkin (2014);
- 1,884 pages of *Stalin: Waiting for Hitler, 1929-1941* (Vol. II), by Prof. Kotkin (2018) [now writing Vol. III, while also serving as Research Scholar, Hoover Institution, Stanford University];
- 816 pages of *Stalin: The Court of the Red Tsar*, by journalist Simon Sebag Montefiore (2003);
- 528 pages of *Young Stalin* by Simon Sebag Montefiore (2007);
- 633 pages of *The Great Terror: Stalin's Purges of the 1930s* by renown historian Robert Conquest, a Senior Research Fellow and Scholar-Curator at Hoover Institution, Stanford University (1968);
- 434 pages of *The Harvest of Sorrow: Soviet Collectivisation and the Terror-Famine* by Robert Conquest (1986);
- 164 pages of *Stalin and the Kirov Murder* by Robert Conquest (1989);
- 368 pages of *Stalin: Breaker of Nations* by Robert Conquest (1991);
- 310 pages of *Stalin: A New History*, edited by UK Prof. Sarah Davies (Durham U.) and Prof. James Harris (U. of Leeds), Cambridge University Press (2005);
- 272 pages of *Stalin's Library: A Dictator and his Books* by Geoffrey Roberts, *emeritus* professor of history at University College Cork, National University of Ireland (2022).

Each of these books got at least two "deep dive" reads from me. Keep in mind that I've always loved studying history and leaders: first as a kid, and then in my undergrad days at the University of Texas at Austin (with the great Prof. Gould, Prof. Farmayan, Prof. Frantz, and many others). Right up to the present, I still deep dive into the best books on the great figures of history and business, learning their rules for winning.

About me.

I got my undergrad degree from University of Texas at Austin, law school degree at Southern Methodist University in Dallas, Texas, and a post-grad in finance management at Wharton School of Business (Aresty Inst. of Executive Education). Then, I applied what I learned from studying the great figures of history. I did this when I started out doing oil & gas deals in south Texas with my mentors Dick Miller and Clint Manges. Later on, I went to Wall Street to do takeovers and proxy contests, such as in 1988 for The Sun Company, a $7.4 billion oil & gas company.

During my time in Wall Street, I met fascinating and highly successful leaders such as the billionaires Boone Pickens, Harold Simmons, and Carl Icahn. I noticed that they used the same Top Ten Rules that Stalin used in his career.

From 1993 to 1995, I went to Utah to do venture capital. I did investment deals with the Eccles Family's First Security bank (now part of Wells Fargo). During my time in venture capital, I got to meet Prof. Stephen Covey and Prof. Clay Christensen along with Ray Noorda, Philippe Kahn, James Sorenson, Jon Huntsman (Sr.), and other highly successful innovators.

From 1989 to 1993, I also authored five publications for Lexis Law Publishing on: federal and state securities law; law of class actions and derivative actions; civil and criminal RICO law (racketeering); and, Law of Collateralized Mortgage & Debt Obligations.

You can read my full bio or profile at https://www.linkedin.com/in/ernestmedsel/

# RULE 1: NEVER SPEAK FIRST, LET OTHERS TALK

Stalin never spoke first. He always let others speak first, especially at meetings. Stalin liked to hear and see what people said and thought. He always let people talk and talk without interruption. This tactic let him find out if a person was for or against him, his ideas, and his plans. He always remembered what they said and later held it over them if necessary (even years later).

When it was his time to speak, Stalin or his closest cronies would *first* ask anyone who had kept silent what they thought on the matter. This way, everyone's words and thoughts were on the record.

When he finally spoke, long after everyone spoke their mind, Stalin would, if necessary, make adjustments on what to say in order to take into account what others had said. Even when he was the undisputed and absolute leader, he always sought a consensus or basic agreement to his ideas and plans from his inner circle and others around him.

After hearing everyone, Stalin now knew who would support him or oppose him and who would help or sabotage his plans. Sometimes, the dictator made changes to his talk or speech in order to get others to feel less threatened by his ideas or plans. Or, Stalin would add or subtract parts of his planned speech or talking points in order to set up people who disliked him or wanted him to fail or be proven wrong.

After hearing everyone first, Stalin figured out what to say and, more important, who was for or against him and his plans.

**Self Assessment Test:** questions to ask yourself if you are going to be highly successful. Some questions are repetitive to drive home an important point.

1. Do you speak first or wait until everyone has spoken at a meeting?

2. Do you pay attention to what people say and think? Do you

write down what they said at the time or shortly later?

3. Do you let people talk and talk without interruption?

4. How do you know if a person is for or against you, your ideas, and your plans?

5. What type of subtle questions can you ask to find out if a person is, or could be, against you, your ideas, or your plans?

6. Do you pay close attention to what a person has said at meetings? How do you remember exactly what was said? Do you write down what was said?

7. Before you speak, do you or a trustworthy ally, *first* ask anyone who was silent on what they think about the topic being discussed?

8. Before you speak, do you make necessary changes that take into account what others have said?

9. Do you seek a consensus or basic agreement to your ideas and plans from your inner circle and others around you? Do you first *listen* and talk to other people to get their agreement *before* you present a plan or idea? Do you first *ask* questions to test a person's feedback to your ideas or plans before making a final presentation?

10. Have you ever been surprised or harmed by someone who kept quiet when you spoke and later claimed or gossiped that they were against your idea or plan because they knew or thought it was bad or flawed?

11. After hearing every person at or before a meeting, do you know who supports you or is against you, your ideas, or your plans?

12. After hearing every person at or before a meeting, do you know who will help you or who will sabotage your ideas and plans?

13. After *first* hearing others, do you make necessary changes

to your talking points in order to get others to feel less threatened by your ideas or plans?

14. Do you change your talking points to take into account any issues or problems that others have pointed out in your ideas or plans?

15. Do your talking points alienate or please the people listening to them?

16. Do you adjust your talking points so no one objects to them at the time?

17. Do you do everything possible to get incremental or "baby step" agreement to your ideas or plans? Do you avoid "take it or leave it" talking points or positions?

## RULE 2: SOCIALIZE, NETWORK, REPEAT

Stalin spent tons of "after hours" time eating, drinking, talking, singing, and socializing with his inner circle, their families, and the people he needed to survive and thrive. He was notorious for all night eat-and-drink binges where his guests got drunk and lost their inhibitions when talking. Their impaired state let him find out exactly what people really thought about him, his ideas and plans, and the people around him.

Stalin used his socializing to network, build alliances, and get people to confess their secrets to him. The dictator watched who liked, disliked, or hated whom. Remember, he listened and rarely spoke. And, he never ever disclosed his real feelings, true intentions or plans, or deepest secrets.

In the post-pandemic "remote" work-from-home office, you will still be able to socialize at mandatory on-site office meetings. If all you can do is a quick coffee break or lunch chat, then start with that. Build on small social interactions since all relationships take time to build, test, and grow.

You will also have good chances of socializing at trade associations, conventions, seminars, and conferences. Like Stalin, make the time and effort to socialize outside of work with co-workers, peers, bosses, clients, and other people you need to succeed.

Even the rich and famous socialize to one degree or the other; or, they pay the consequences.

Take Steve Jobs at Apple. Although rich and famous, he never socialized with the board of directors. Nor did he keep tabs on them after he brought in John Sculley, the Pepsi CEO, to help run Apple in 1983.

Sculley, a long-time "professional manager," was skilled in schmoozing, corporate double-talk, and corporate-speak. Mr. Pepsi was supposed to bring "professional" focus and "big corporation" discipline to Apple. Smooth-talking and polished-mannered Sculley was also supposed to offset the awful social skills of Steve Jobs, whose atrocious anti-social people skills included bullying, screaming, temper tantrums, etc.

Guess what?

Sculley got the board of directors to fire Apple co-founder Steve Jobs two years later, in 1985.

How?

Incremental socializing with key members of the board of directors.

Sculley did a Stalin, slowly over time, until the board demanded that Steve Jobs resign. Of course, it all turned out well for Steve Jobs.

Jobs came back to Apple in 1997 after Sculley proved that he was only a corporate bureaucrat and an MBA whose only expertise was marketing. Sculley's career consisted of working at Marschalk, a Madison Avenue ad agency. Then, at Pepsi/Frito-Lay, he was in charge of marketing soda and chips (tortilla and potato chips, not computer chips).

**Self Assessment Test:** questions to ask yourself if you are going to be highly successful. Some questions repeat to emphasize a point.

1. Do I spend "after hours" time socializing with people I need for success in my career or business?

2. Do I truly listen and carefully watch what people say and do at social events with people I need for my career or business?

3. At social events with people I need for my career or business, do I make sure that I listen, ask, and find out exactly what people really think about me, my ideas and plans, and the people around me?

4. When I socialize with people I need for my career or business, do I socialize to make friends or pass the time? Or, do I socialize to network, build alliances, and get people to confess their plans and deep secrets to me?

5. Do I know how to ask questions to get people to tell me their real plans? Their deepest secrets? Do I know how to keep my plans secrets and deepest secrets even more secret? Do I know how to offer information to others that makes them think that they know my real plans or deepest secrets without me revealing my true intentions or personal secrets? [Stalin was a master at this thanks to his years in seminary, confessing to the priests just enough to make the priests happy, while also snitching on other students he disliked or hated].

5. When I socialize with people I need for my career or business, do I watch and listen to find out who likes, dislikes, or hates whom?

6. When I socialize with people I need for my career or business, do I mostly listen and rarely speak (and when I speak, I only ask questions)?

7. When I socialize with people I need for my career or business, do I disclose my real feelings, plans, or deepest secrets?

8. Do you have the social skills and people skills to socialize with people, even with total strangers?

9. If socializing is hard for you, what can you do to mix and interact with people if you're in a career or business that needs networking and allies?

10. If you're shy or have little or no social skills, have you considered the Dale Carnegie book *How to Win Friends and Influence People*?

# RULE 3: WORK TO THE MAX

Stalin worked like crazy: non-stop and, if necessary, to the physical maximum every day. He was the ultimate workhorse who could be counted on to carry out any job. That's why Lenin, the leader, depended on him. None of his rivals and peers had the discipline or focus to work so hard. Ten and twelve hour work days were the rule for Stalin, not the exception.

As soon as he joined the Communist Party, Stalin put in endless hours. His jobs ranged from being the editor of the party's Pravda newspaper to acting as a military commander in the 1919-1921 war against Poland.

Stalin's clever ability to mix with people, and read them like a book, led to his appointment as Commissar of Nationalities. In this important post, he helped the communists rule over the many ethnic, racial, and language minorities of Russia.

Stalin's devoted "true believer" loyalty caught the eye of Lenin, the leader, who then appointed him General Secretary of the Communist Party. Lenin also rewarded Stalin for his solid work ethic (never complaining or bragging).

As General Secretary, Stalin completed all sorts of boring, difficult, and time-consuming tasks. He soon controlled access to Lenin, while he did the "dirty" and controversial work that no one else wanted to do for Lenin. The job allowed Stalin to learn and mange every detail of governing Russia, a giant country. He also got to supervise and appoint every important post in the party *and* the government.

Think about it, Russia is spread across eleven time zones (yes, 11) and filled with dozens and dozens of of nationalities, ethnic groups, religions, and languages. And yet, Stalin made the time to read and respond to everything that came across his desk. He even read and approved newspaper articles, school books, party propaganda, movie scripts, plays, and poems.

Tens of thousands of documents (letters, memos, orders) contain his handwritten marks and comments, and signature, showing that he read every one of them, including lists of thousands of people to be arrested and executed.

**Self Assessment Test:** questions to ask yourself if you are going to be highly successful.

1. Do you speak first or wait until everyone has spoken at a meeting?

2. Do you pay attention to what people say and think? Do you write down what they said at the time or shortly later?

3. Do you let people talk and talk without interruption?

4. Do you know if a person is for or against you, your ideas, and your plans?

5. What type of subtle questions can you ask to find out if a person is, or could be, against you, your ideas, or your plans?

6. Do you pay close attention to what a person has said at business meetings? Do you remember exactly what was said? Do you write down what was said?

# RULE 4: BE INDISPENSABLE, IGNORE THE INGRATES

Without a doubt, Stalin worked like crazy. But he expected no gratitude in return from anyone, least of all from his boss, Lenin.

First, Stalin worked hard without expecting gratitude in order to become *the* "go to guy" if anyone wanted anything done. In other words, he became *indispensable*, absolutely necessary, to his boss Lenin, his peers, the Communist Party, and the government itself. Stalin did this even when he was the absolute and undisputed top leader.

Second, Stalin worked like crazy without expecting gratitude so he could meet every single person who would help his career and plans. This "fan base" would owe him a favor for his work, which he might or might not collect down the road (to test a person's gratitude and loyalty). This is the perfect method to let you find out if you have a loyal "fan" or a disloyal ingrate in a boss, peer, co-worker, client, or other person you need to succeed.

Third, Stalin never retaliated or lashed out in anger when he found an ingrate. Instead, the smart operator bid his time until he could get rid of the ingrate.

Fourth, Stalin worked like a maniac without expecting gratitude so he could put his finger in every pie and learn every aspect of the party and government he wanted to rule and own.

In a nutshell, in order to succeed, Stalin worked beyond hard in order to become *indispensable* to his boss Lenin, the Communist Party, and the government itself.

At the same time, Stalin expected no gratitude from his bosses. He famously said:

"Only dogs are grateful."

Stalin's realistic expectations came true when he found out that Lenin's last will and testament attacked him along with a string of criticisms. Lenin's will threatened to put an end to Stalin's career. So did his enemies, and Lenin's widow, who hated him.

But, by the time Lenin died, the General Secretary had become the one indispensable "go to guy" who had allies everywhere in the party, military, secret police, and government thanks to his rules:

# 1. Never speak first and only listen;
# 2. Socialize a lot, but never reveal your true intentions, plans, or real feelings;
# 3. Work like crazy;
# 4. Become indispensable without expecting gratitude.

You will never be disappointed, angry, or upset when you do *not* expect gratitude from anyone, especially when you're working like crazy, beyond expectations, to do a job well done. This attitude and strategy lets you, like Stalin, objectively and coldly find out:

- who is grateful or not;
- who is or is not dependable and loyal to you;
- who likes or dislikes you;
- who wants to help or sabotage you.

**Self Assessment Test:** questions to ask yourself if you are going to be highly successful.

1. Do you work like crazy, but expect no gratitude in return from anyone, least of all from your boss?

2. Do you work hard without expecting gratitude in order to become *the* "go to guy" if anyone wants anything done?

3. Do you work hard to become *indispensable*, absolutely necessary, to your boss, peers, co-workers, clients, and anyone else?

4. Do you work like a maniac in order to meet every single person who might, could, or will help your career and plans?

5. Do you keep track of each person who owes you a favor for your help or your work? Do you test a person's gratitude and loyalty to find out if they're real "fans" of yours?

6. What do you do to find out if you have a loyal "fan" or a disloyal ingrate in a boss, peer, co-worker, client, or other person you need to succeed?

7. Do you retaliate or get upset when you find an ingrate in your boss, peers, co-workers, clients, or other persons you need to succeed? Do you bide your time until you can get rid of the ingrate?

8. Do you work hard without expecting gratitude so you can learn and master every aspect of the job, career, business, or company that you want to rule or own?

9. Do you *not* expect gratitude from anyone when you work like crazy in order to find out, sooner or later:
- who is grateful or not?
- who is or is not dependable and loyal to you?
- who likes or dislikes you?
- who wants to help or sabotage you?

10. Do you work very hard to please others (in the short term) or do you work hard to lay the groundwork for your success (in the long term)?

11. Do you get angry, upset, or blindsided if your boss, peers, clients, or other people are not grateful for your hard work or do not appreciate it? Do you understand that most people are not grateful for what you do for them?

12. Do you go out of your way every single day to deliver top results without caring about anyone's gratitude or appreciation (while also keeping score of who is/was grateful and loyal)?

## RULE 5: TEST AND REPLACE PEOPLE

During his entire life, Stalin constantly tested the people around him. He tested people by working and socializing with them and paying close attention to what they said or did. Remember, he let them talk and talk to him and others (who then reported back to him). Stalin also tested the people he needed for his plans by asking them for small favors (like promoting someone) or making subtle and trivial suggestions (like playing a song).

Sooner or later, after testing the people he needed, Stalin replaced them if they failed any of his tests. He replaced bosses, friends, allies, peers, co-workers, underlings, and everyone else at home and at work. While Stalin worked very hard to become indispensable, he also made sure that no one was indispensable to him.

Stalin knew that you lose your freedom when you depend on any one person for your career, profession, or business. It's a cold hard reality that each of us depends on one or more persons to help our career or plans, just like Stalin depended on Lenin. But the former seminary student knew that he had to keep "dependency" to anyone at a minimum and for the shortest time possible.

Stalin always took his time to test and replace the people he needed to win. As Lenin got sicker and weaker with strokes, Stalin laid the groundwork for the day when Lenin would die. Stalin concentrated power to himself as he made more and more decisions for his badly disabled boss. Stalin also started to exclude Lenin from decisions. And, he set up a ton of alliances, like with Zinoviev and Kamenev, to get rid of his biggest rival, Leon Trotsky.

After Trotsky fled from Russia, Stalin bid his time until he was secure enough to go after his former allies, Zinoviev and Kamenev. First, he demoted them or expelled them from the Communist Party. Later on, he put them on trial and had them shot during the Great Terror (or Great Purges) of the 1930s.

During the Great Terror, Stalin used Genrikh Yagoda, the chief of the secret police (the NKVD, later the KGB). Yagoda's NKVD got rid of every person who did or might oppose Stalin. This meant execution or the concentration camps of the Gulag.

Three years later, Stalin replaced Yagoda with Nikolai Yezhov, the #2 at the NKVD, which arrested and executed Yagoda. Less than four years later, Stalin replaced Yezhov with Lavrenti Beria, who dispatched Yezhov the same way.

At the time of his death, Stalin was already planning another purge to replace people around him.

On a daily basis until his death, Stalin took inventory of the people he needed for his career, plans, and success. The inventory came from constantly meeting people, working and socializing with them, and finding out if they were:
- loyal and reliable or predictable (like life-long associates Kaganovich, Kruschev, Molotov, and Voroshilov); or,
- hostile to him or his ideas and plans, unpredictable, or too independent (like Bukharin, Ordzhonikidze, and Rykov).

Sooner or later, Stalin replaced anyone and everyone who was hostile, wavering, unpredictable, or too independent.

You need to keep Stalin Rule No. 5 in mind because bosses, peers, co-workers, clients, vendors, and allies will betray and turn on productive, loyal, and talented people, like you, who work hard. Stalin Rule No. 5 applies no matter what kind of career, profession, or work you pursue.

You proceed at your own risk if you do not plan on how and when to replace your boss, peers, co-workers, clients, vendors, or allies after they have proved that they're hostile, disloyal, ungrateful, or unpredictable. If not, you risk them finding a replacement for you. This might even require you getting a new job or career before they replace you.

**Self Assessment Test:** questions to ask yourself if you are going to be highly successful.

1. Do you constantly test the people around you (by asking them for small favors such as giving you vacation time or medical leave, help with a project, or advice on a work matter)?

2. Do you test your bosses, friends, allies, peers, co-workers, underlings, and others at work to find out if they are loyal, reliable, and predictable? Or, if they are hostile, disloyal, ungrateful, or unpredictable?

3. Are you ready to replace your bosses, friends, allies, peers, co-workers, underlings, and others you need for your career or business if they are hostile, disloyal, unpredictable, or ungrateful? How will you do the replacing? What specific plans do you have if they are hostile, disloyal, unpredictable, or ungrateful?

4. Do you work hard to constantly find out if the people you need for your success are loyal, reliable, and predictable? Or, if they're hostile to you or your ideas and plans? Or, are they unpredictable or too independent?

5. Which boss, peer, co-worker, client, vendor, or ally could, will, or might betray you or replace you?

# RULE 6: FIGHT THE WEAK, NOT THE STRONG

Stalin always looked for the weakest point(s) in his competition and competitors. He then attacked those weak points without mercy. He never picked a fight with any actual or possible competition (or competitor) that was strong. No winner in business, politics, or war ever got to the top by attacking the strongest points(s) of a competitor.

For example, Stalin never picked a fight with Nadezhda, Lenins' wife, who hated him. He never verbally attacked or openly criticized her until the very end, when Lenin was disabled and dying. And, he left her alone, but isolated and powerless, after Lenin died, because she was too popular to arrest, jail, or execute.

Stalin was smart in never going after someone as strong as Nadezhda. Almost everyone loved or respected Lenin's wife, and then widow, because they liked her and/or loved her husband. Any attack or criticism on Nadezhda would've been seen as treason and an attack or criticism on the revered Lenin himself.

Stalin always searched for and found the weakest point in his competitors. He did this because, first, he never spoke about anything that could later be held or used against him; and, second, he always let the competition, and the people he needed to win, talk and talk so he could find and point out their weakest point(s).

For example, Stalin used Rule No. 6 on his arch-rival. The arrogant Trotsky had the bad habit of insulting people to their faces, always showing off his superior intelligence, and making others look bad. Stalin carefully studied Trotsky's weak points. He then used them to gain allies and turn people against Trotsky.

The seminary dropout did the same to:
- his peers (Zinoviev; Kamenev; Bukharin; Ordzhonikidze; Rykov);
- his killer henchmen (Yagoda; Yezhov); and,
- even a top general like Tukhachevsky.

They all ended up losing to Stalin and dead.

Stalin also applied Rule No. 6 to his close allies, like Beria, Kaganovich, Kruschev, Molotov, and Voroshilov. He always brought up their weak points to keep them docile, humble, and obedient. Stalin also brought up their weak points against each other in order to keep them divided, either suspicious of each other or loathing and hating each other.

**Self Assessment Test:** questions to ask yourself if you are going to be highly successful.

1. When dealing with the competition, do you work hard to find their weakest point(s)?

2. After you find the weakest point(s) of your competition or competitors, how do you use that against them?

3. Do you remind people of the worst weak points of your competition?

4. Do you focus on reminding people about a competitor's weak point, which they also happen to really dislike or hate?

# RULE 7: LEARN ALL YOU CAN ALL THE TIME

Not only did Stalin work like crazy and socialize a lot, but he also read a lot. He was a self-educated expert in: world history, especially Russian history; and, communist theory and thought, especially those of Karl Marx and Vladimir Lenin (his boss).

Although he made it a crime to read or discuss the thoughts and ideas of Leon Trotsky, Stalin secretly studied the books and writings of his peer, rival, and arch-enemy (both before and after Stalin ordered Trotsky's murder in Mexico, where Leon had escaped).

Stalin read all he could about his enemies, like Hitler, and allies, like Churchill and Roosevelt. He also read novels, plays, and poetry.

Stalin read all he could from books, magazines, studies, and reports to make sure that he was not being misled by any expert in any field, especially in the military, business, finance, trade, industry, or the economy.

Prof. Kotkin calls Stalin the ultimate *autodidact* (a self-taught genius).

Historians discovered that Stalin's personal library had 25,000 books, which he had read, underlined, and marked-up with notes and comments over the decades. A separate building housed the books next to his favorite dacha, ten miles from the Kremlin, in the Kuntsevo suburb.

Stalin had his own private librarian (Lenin's). The former seminarian personally wrote up a catalog of all of the books that he had read, along with a summary of the topics that they contained. Stalin even died in his library or study at the Kuntsevo dacha.

From his youth until his death at age 74, Stalin always kept learning by reading a lot. He rose to the very top even though he was the equivalent of a college dropout. He kept learning on his own, building on his excellent education as a seminary candidate who only needed to pass the final exam to become a priest.

Stalin memorized all of Lenin's books and writings. He became an expert on Marxist-Leninist communism. He could out-argue anyone when it came to socialism and communism.

By sheer will power, and hard work, Stalin became the intellectual "torch bearer" and "heir" of Lenin. This gave him legitimacy in the party and the government in his rise to absolute rule. As an expert on Lenin and Marx, he had street cred (credentials) with regular people and party members. The former priest-to-be became a true believer in communism, which required fanatics to do many and terrible things for lofty goals of an equal society with shared property.

By studying Marx and Lenin, Stalin became an evangelist for communism. He led other true believers into leaving millions dead and imprisoned in a world of famine, mass murder, total dictatorship, and the world's largest network of concentration camps, the Gulag. The historian Robert Conquest estimates at least 20 million dead thanks to Stalin orders and policies. Only Mao in China surpassed this death toll.

No other world leaders have killed more of their own people than Stalin and Mao.

How?

By the control of ideas to influence and control people.

Going back to the *Steve Jobs v. John Sculley* war at Apple, please note that unlike Steve Jobs, the former Pepsi CEO, John Sculley, never took the time and effort to educate himself on computers, tech, or any details about Apple's business, culture, clients, vendors, employees, software, and hardware. Sculley focused on handling the board of directors and marketing Apple products. During his 10-year tenure as CEO, Sculley had no real idea why clients want to buy Apple products.

The result?

Apple stock dived low in penny stock territory. The board of directors forced him out after 10 years living off products started by Steve Jobs.

Until his early death, Steve Jobs was a master of explaining his ideas of technology and the customer. Like Stalin, he was an evangelist who created true believers of Apple products. In fact, Apple was the first tech company to create the official job title of Chief Evangelist (for Guy Kawasaki, preacher of Macintosh). Nowadays every company wants "influencers" preaching their brand on social media.

**Self Assessment Test:** questions to ask yourself if you are going to be highly successful.

1.  How well do you know your business, trade, profession, or career?

2.  Are you an expert in your business, trade, profession, or career? [Note: you don't have to be the very best; but, like Stalin, you have to know the basics.]

3.  If you can't read a lot or don't like to read, have you tried listening to audio books while you commute or travel?

4.  Do you study what your boss, peers, or rivals know about your business, trade, profession, or career? Is your knowledge less than, the same, or greater than what they know?

5.  How easily could you be misled or misinformed by any expert in any field, especially an expert in your business, trade, profession, or career?

6.  Do you know everything, a lot, or a little about what there is to know about your business, trade, profession or career?

7.  Did you know that your control or use of an idea lets you influence or control people?

8.  What idea or ideas do you have that would allow you to influence or control people you need for your career, job, work, or profession?

# RULE 8: ALWAYS JUMP INTO THE NEW

Stalin was never afraid of jumping into new activities, new jobs, new careers.

Stalin didn't care if he was or was not qualified or experienced. Nor did Stalin care if he was the best or the worst at the new job or career. He didn't even care if his performance was mediocre or average.

Long before Nike made the saying popular, Stalin was living the motto: "Just do it."

One thing was for sure: Stalin did the new job or career with gusto, jumping "all in" to his newest venture. Stalin jumped into no less than 12 jobs or careers, in the following order:
- seminary student and priest candidate doing God's work;
- weatherman;
- Marxist communist rebel using violence to get rid of churches, religion, the Czar, private property, and the government;
- terrorist who organized the botched Tiflis bank robbery of 1907, killing 40, injuring 50;
- newspaper editor for Pravda;
- author and editor of political pamphlets and books on Marxist communism;
- political commissar in the Red Army during the war with Poland (1919-1921);
- Commissar of Nationalities, which put him in charge of imposing Russian and communist rule over ethnic minorities like his own;
- General Secretary of the Communist Party;
- Economic and Financial Planner behind the Five Year Plan system that ruled the Russian economy from 1928 to 1995 with a total of thirteen Five Year Plans (Stalin personally created the first three plans, which forced Russia to change from a backward farm economy into a modern factory economy);
- Military and War Planner (strategy and tactics);
- International Relations and Geopolitical Strategy with major world powers, such as Germany, Japan, China, the USA, France, and

England.

Stalin had some huge failures in his twelve jobs and careers. You will see them in the next rule, Rule No. 9 ("Embrace Your Failure"). And yet, the seminary dropout not only rose to the very top, but he also stayed at the top for 30 years.

**Self Assessment Test:** questions to ask yourself if you are going to be highly successful.

1. Are you afraid of jumping into new activities, new jobs, or new careers?

2. Would you reject a chance at a new activity, job, or career because, in your mind, you're not qualified or experienced enough? Have you done this in the past?

3. What opportunities have you turned down or abandoned because you thought that you would be the worst (or not the best) at the new job or career?

4. Do you turn down opportunities because you worry that you would be mediocre or average?

5. Does the motto "Just do it" apply to your career, job, profession, or business?

6. Do you say yes to opportunities and then do the new activity, job, or career with enthusiasm?

7. If you are the very best in your job, isn't that actually going to keep you forever in that job, especially if you're not the owner or boss?

Remember, the saddest thought is "I wish I had done that." The great American poet, John Greenleaf Whittier, hit the nail on the head when he wrote:
"For all sad words of tongue and pen, the saddest are these, *It might have been.*"

Don't be your own worst boss or enemy. Promote yourself when you get the chance.

Be like Stalin: his only regret was that he had no regrets.

# RULE 9: EMBRACE YOUR FAILURES: LEARN FROM THEM

Stalin had huge failures and some success in many if not most of his 12 jobs or careers. And yet, he made it to the top and stayed there for 30 years.

- He failed as a seminary student and priest candidate.

- He failed as a weatherman.

- He was good as a Marxist communist rebel using violence to get rid of churches, religion, the Czar, private property, and the government.

- He was a failed terrorist in charge of the botched Tiflis bank robbery of 1907 that killed 40 and wounded 50.

- He was good as a newspaper editor for Pravda.

- He was good as an author and editor of political pamphlets and books on Marxist communism. His own written works add up to 16 volumes, from 1901 to 1952.

- He was a disaster as a commissar in the Red Army during the war in 1919-1921 with Poland. Stalin and General Yegorov disobeyed orders from Lenin and Trotsky. Their disobedience prevented an all-out attack on Warsaw. Russia lost the war. Stalin was never really blamed because he had opposed the war from the start. A rarity for him, Stalin spoke out early against the war since he knew it was doomed to fail.

- He was good as Commissar of Nationalities, imposing Russian and communist rule over ethnic minorities like his own.

- He was very good as General Secretary of the Communist

Party.

- Millions died from starvation in Ukraine thanks to his Five Year Plan to force farmers and peasants into state-owned collectives.

- Mass poverty, scarcity, and rationing was the price everyone paid for Stalin's Five Year Plans that forced the entire country to change from a backward agrarian economy into a modern industrial state. Of course, the communist elites enjoyed comfortable lifestyles.

- Stalin failed to see that Hitler would invade Russia instead of invading England. Hitler's Germany would have conquered Russia but for Stalin having forced his country to become a modern industrial nation. Hitler later admitted that he had no idea that Russia could make so many tanks.

- Stalin was a total failure in military matters when he ignored his generals and acted as *the* Military and War Planner. By 1939, Stalin was the undisputed leader when he led Russia into a colossal defeat in Finland. A smaller and weaker army of Finland won a winter war from November 1939 to March 1940. The defeat encouraged Hitler to attack Russia in June 1941.

- Stalin had a mixed record with International Relations and Geopolitical Strategy.

- Stalin was smart when dealing with Japan and China. He always came out ahead dealing with Roosevelt and Churchill. On the other hand, Stalin completely misread Hitler in 1939, when they divided Poland and other countries between Germany and Russia.

- Stalin, who read people like books, refused to believe that Hitler would invade Russia. Even though he was a master of paranoia, Stalin refused to believe the many warning signs that Germany would attack.

- Stalin had a blind spot for Hitler and Germany. He thought they were rational and smart players who would first finish off the British by invading England.

- Stalin failed to apply Rule No. 5, *Test & Replace People*, to his alliance with Hitler and Germany. Stalin failed to see how Hitler could not even destroy the British army when they were trapped at Dunkirk in France.

- Stalin's failures almost led to Hitler and Germany winning. Stalin's purges and terror had decimated Russian society and the military, from top to bottom. German troops moved deep inside Russia. They reached Moscow, St. Petersburg (Leningrad), and Volgograd (Stalingrad). Hitler would have won but for his dallying in 1941, when he was unable to set military priorities, distracted by so many possible victories. The giant territory and brutal weather of Russia sealed the fate of Hitler and Germany. So did massive help from the USA.

- Stalin's blind failures with Hitler and Germany are odd given that paranoid Stalin always schemed against and killed off his rivals, former allies, and even his in-laws. But, by June 22, 1941, when Hitler attacked, Joe Stalin had become 100% indispensable to the people, government, and military of Russia. The country had no one else to lead the war thanks to Rule No. 5, *Test & Replace People*. Stalin ruthlessly applied Rule No. 5 inside Russia to Russians. He enjoyed the ultimate job and career security thanks to Rule No. 5, which got rid of all internal opposition to him and his ideas.

**Self Assessment Test:** questions to ask yourself if you are going to be highly successful.

1. Have you had small or big failures in many, if not most, of your activities, jobs, or careers?

2. Have you failed in school or in getting the right education?

3. Ever been fired or forced out of a job? Made big mistakes in your work or career?

3. Do you allow past failure(s) in your activities, job, or career to stop you from doing more in life or from jumping into a new

activity, job, or career?

4. Do your past failure(s) stop you from winning in life? Or, do your past failure(s) stop you from *thinking* you can win?

5. When you make a mental list of your small or big failures, do you also make a list of your small or big wins?

6. What weak point(s) do you have that led to your small or big failure(s)?

7. What are you going to do to fix *your* weak point(s), which led to your small or big failure(s)?

8. What have you learned from each of your small or big failure(s)?

9. Have you made up your mind to win despite any failure(s) in your past?

Be like Stalin, get over your failures. Learn from them. Pain and failure are the greatest teachers. Henry Ford and Walt Disney failed before winning. Both lost their first company before hitting the big time.
Use the other rules to win no matter what failure lurks in your past or in your mind.
Failure never wins when you are 100% indispensable in your work, job, or career.

# RULE 10: WRONG PLACE, WRONG TIME, NO PROBLEM

Stalin spent a lifetime being in the wrong place at the wrong time. And yet, he rose to the top.

He was not born to wealth, power, or privilege with the educated elites of big cities like Moscow or into the aristocracy of the Czar's court. Quite the opposite: Stalin began as Ioseb (or Iosif) Dzhugashvili at the bottom of the social and economic ladder. Few would expect much from a pock-marked and poverty-stricken kid born to an ethnic minority in a remote province.

His parents? A brutal drunk cobbler of a father who, when not beating them up, abandoned him and his mother. But, the religious Keke was a maid with street smarts and ambition for her only son. She got a rich, well-connected man to pay for his education as a priest.

Stalin dropped out of Tiflis Theological Seminary, where his revolutionary anti-Czar activities got him kicked out. After less than a year, he left his only paying job at the weather observatory in Tiflis.

Without a doubt, Stalin was born in the wrong place at the wrong time.

For the next 13 years, from 1900 to 1913, Stalin was a low-level member of the opposition underground. He joined the Marxist rebels in the Social Democratic party. When the party split in 1903, Stalin went with the radical and violent minority, or Bolshevik, faction led by Lenin.

No one expected Lenin and his followers to ever get to power. The Bolsheviks had less than 25,000 members in the Czar's empire of 125 million subjects. After 4 years in prison and exile, Lenin spent the next 17 years outside of Russia (except from 1905 to 1907 when he went back to fail again at overthrowing the Czar).

As a boss working remote in safety from far away, Lenin loved Stalin's non-stop work and his absolute loyalty and obedience. Stalin's devotion to Lenin meant that Stalin paid dearly: he spent the next 13 years as a wanted criminal. Stalin got arrested, jailed, convicted, and sent to exile in Siberia. He went through a spin cycle of "escape-and-recapture" several times until 1917.

No doubt, Stalin was living in the wrong place at the wrong time.

Stalin, Lenin, and the Bolsheviks got caught by surprise when the Czar abdicated and was removed from power. His reign ended when mass protests and food riots broke out in 1916-1917. Russians were enraged over the Czar's incompetence while he was also losing the war to Germany during World War I.

Stalin, Lenin, and the Bolsheviks had little to do with the overthrow of the government. In fact, the Germans, eager to destroy Russia and the Czar, allowed Lenin to travel in a secret train from Switzerland to Russia. So, it was the German military that opened the way for Lenin, Stalin, and the Bolsheviks to hijack the Russian Revolution against the Czar. Thanks to Germany, Lenin, Stalin, and cohorts took over Russia by being the most ruthless and focused rebels.

Keep in mind that the fall of the Czar came from Russia's weak points: the inflated hubris of the Czar; ruling class delusions of competence; and, the elite's wishful thinking. Nicholas II led Russia straight into the disaster called World War I when he joined the West (England, France, USA) against Germany and the Austria-Hungary Empire.

It's clear that Stalin was living in the wrong place at the wrong time. After all, Lenin and his cohorts were, at most, insignificant nobodies in the political landscape after the Czar fell.

Stalin, Lenin, and the Bolsheviks then used Stalin Rule No. 6 (Find & Fight the Weak, Not the Strong) against their competition and the provisional government that took over after the Czar abdicated. Rule No. 6 allowed them to hijack the revolution and take over Russia during the power vacuum and confusion that existed after Czar Nicholas II abdicated.

Within a short time of Lenin's arrival in Russia on April 16, 1917, the Bolsheviks grew to a total of about 250,000 members. That's impressive, but still less than 2% in a country with a population of 125 million. And yet, they took over Russia, just the same way that only a small minority of Americans wanted a revolution against the British in 1776.

In the early hours of July 17, 1918, the communists executed Nicholas II and his family. A civil war was also raging between the Red Army (led by Trotsky) and the White armies until 1922, when Lenin's Reds finally won the war. And just like that, Russia was under the brutal rule of Stalin, Lenin, and the communists.

Stalin, Lenin, and cohorts had all been born and living in the wrong place and the wrong time until 1914. They had been ruined and disgraced when they tried fighting the powerful system of the Czar, the courts, the wealthy, and the secret police, the pervasive Okhrana.

But the Czar had three weak points: a lenient form of letting political prisoners live comfortably in civilian homes while in exile; empty dreams of winning an unwinnable war; and, delusions of competent governing. These weak points undid Nicholas II and cost him his life along with that of his wife and their five children.

By 1918, Stalin, Lenin, and the communists were on their way to win big time thanks to the weak points of the Czar and his supporters. Stalin, Lenin, and their cohorts used Stalin's Rule No. 6 to win and do the impossible (despite all of them being born and living in the wrong place at the wrong time).

Trotsky was hailed and admired as the man who led the Red Army to victory; he was the heir to Lenin; and yet, Stalin outsmarted him by going after the man's weak points and using all of his ten rules against Trotsky.

No matter how bad your situation is, or how you've always been in the wrong place and the wrong time since birth, Stalin's Rule No. 10 is for you to always keep pressing forward and using all the other rules in order to finally win.

Like a surfer, you have to wait for the tides of history and the waves of change to bring you closer to your ultimate goal or goals. Or, as Edward James Olmos famously said when giving some great advice:

"That's me, that's you, drops of water . . . and you think, Wait a minute, I'm a mountain top water drop. I don't belong in this valley, this river, this low dark ocean....

"But then one day it gets hot, and you slowly evaporate into air, way up, higher than any mountain top, all the way into the heavens....

"Life's a journey that goes round and round.... So if it's change you need, relish the journey. Be a drop of water and relish those invisible pulls of your soul."

**Self Assessment Test:** questions to ask yourself if you are going to be highly successful.

1. Were you born in the wrong place at the wrong time?

2. Did you grow up in the wrong place at the wrong time?

3. Do you have little or no education or connections?

4. Are you living or working in the wrong place at the wrong time?

5. Have you made a list of all the things that are wrong with your life?

6. Have you made a list of the weak points of the competition and your competitors?

7. What plan do you have to use those weak points to your advantage?

8. What are you doing to benefit from the weak points of your competitors? Will you win if you execute your plan(s) to benefit from those weak points?

9. Are you always pressing and pushing forward by using all of Stalin's rules to win?

10. Do you have the patience and ability to wait for time and change to bring you the chances and opportunities that you need to win?

# CONCLUSION

Stalin rose to the very top and stayed there for 30 years.

He came from the wrong side of the tracks. During his 18 years as a young adult (age 21 to age 39 from 1899 to 1917), Stalin was a misfit, an outcast, a convicted criminal, wanted felon, and a total failure in his priest education and career. In other words, a loser.

In middle age, from age 40 to age 63 (1917-1941), Stalin had many huge failures along with some wins. But he kept applying his rules against far smarter and more popular rivals.

Hitler's invasion in 1941 almost destroyed Stalin and Russia. But he kept applying his rules to turn the tide and win.

At the end of World War Two, at age 67, Stalin ruled more people than any Czar. He went on to make Russia a nuclear superpower in his senior years, from age 64 until he died in his library at age 74 in 1953.

Study the rules and take the tests for each rule.

If you're going to win at work, a job, a career, or any worthwhile activity, you need the Top Ten Rules that Stalin used to win. When he didn't follow the 10 rules, Stalin paid dearly with failure.

Ignore the rules at your own risk.

Rule No. 1:   NEVER SPEAK FIRST, LET OTHERS TALK.

Rule No. 2:   SOCIALIZE, NETWORK, REPEAT.

Rule No. 3:   WORK TO THE MAX.

Rule No. 4:   BE INDISPENSABLE, IGNORE THE INGRATES.

Rule No. 5:   TEST AND REPLACE PEOPLE.

Rule No. 6:   FIGHT THE WEAK, NOT THE STRONG.

Rule No. 7:   LEARN ALL YOU CAN ALL THE TIME.

Rule No. 8:   ALWAYS JUMP INTO THE NEW.

Rule No. 9:   EMBRACE YOUR FAILURES: LEARN FROM THEM.

Rule No. 10:   WRONG PLACE, WRONG TIME, NO PROBLEM.

# CORE COMPETENCE:
# FINAL SELF-ASSESSMENT TEST

Welcome to the final self-assessment test. The exam will test your core competence.

Why? Because deep inside the core of Stalin's Top 10 Rules, two rules are the most useful and powerful.

First, there's Rule No. 5 (*Test And Replace People*).

Second, there's Rule No. 6 (*Fight The Weak, Not The Strong*).

If you can master the use of these two rules, then you will be on your way to winning in your chosen job, work, activity, or career. Think of them the same way that chess players value two pieces the most — the Queen and the Rook. Think of these two rules as the ultimate insurance that protects all of your work and efforts.

Be like Stalin on Rule No. 5 and No. 6 to win in life.

**Final Self-Assessment Test: your core competence (Rule 5 and Rule 6).**

1. Do you know how to protect yourself and your work?

**Competence on Rule No. 5 (*Test And Replace People*).**

2. Do you think that everyone loves you and is on your side, rooting for you? If yes, then stop taking the test and go lose big time.

3. Do you think that there might be some, even your friends, family, co-workers, peers, boss(es), competitors, or competition, who want to see you fail?

4. Can you name five or ten of your friends, family, co-workers, peers, boss(es), competitors, or competition who want you to fail?

5. How do you know who is or might be openly or secretly

against you, your ideas, or your work?

6. How do you test people to find out if they are secretly against you, your ideas, or your work? How often do you test them to find out? When was the last time you tested them? Can you use a better test for them?

7. Can you name five or ten of your friends, family, co-workers, peers, boss(es), competitors, or competition who are against you, your ideas, or your work?

8. Can you name five or ten friends, family, co-workers, peers, or boss(es) that you replaced the past 1, 2, or 3 years because they were against you, your ideas, or your work?

**Competence on Rule No. 6 (*Fight The Weak, Not The Strong*).**

9. What are the five biggest failures in your job, work or career?

10. What are your five weakest points that resulted in your five biggest failures?

Bonus question: what are you doing and have done to fix your weak points?

www.ingramcontent.com/pod-product-compliance
Lightning Source LLC
Chambersburg PA
CBHW072006210526
45479CB00003B/1080